Coming soor

More in the Freshly Baked Con......................
by Lauren Young

Stir

Watch

Serve

Marketing **Success** Starts with
the **Right Ingredients**

Pour

LAUREN YOUNG

Writers of the Round Table Press

1421 PRESS

1421 PRESS

www.pourstirwatchserve.com
www.writersoftheroundtable.com
Cover design, illustrations and layout by Ben Olson,
3 Monkeys & Aardvark Studios

Printed and bound in the U.S.A.
ISBN: 9781937443023
Library of Congress Control Number: 2011916349

To The Other L. Young,
for your eternal sarcasm and love

What's Inside

Foreword

I started traveling around giving keynote speeches in 2007, at the same time I started my first company. Since the company color was orange, I almost exclusively wore an orange button-down shirt, jeans, and a black jacket. I did this for the first five speeches.

For some reason, on the sixth keynote, I decided to wear black. I'm not sure why, I just felt like it.

After that presentation, three people came up to me and asked me what was wrong, and why wasn't I wearing orange.

At that moment, I realized that the color orange was one of my ingredients for business success. Those three people had identified my company, as well as me, with the color orange. That was part of our brand, like the swoosh is a part of Nike's brand or the Apple a part of, well, Apple.

The Right Ingredients

As marketers and business owners, we often think that it's about one thing: our product, our service, our business cards, our retail store, our website, etc. As Lauren points out so well in "Pour: Marketing Success Starts with the Right Ingredients," it's never about one thing.

Orange is part of my success as a business owner. We knew this because we listened to our customers. We paid attention. It's part of us getting their attention.

But that is just a start. As Lauren points out so well in the following pages, the key to dominating your category is by engaging them in every way possible with those ingredients. Let's face it, your customers really don't care about you. They care about themselves. Since that is 100% the case, what can you do as a business to get on their radar?

Listening to your customers is just step one. The key is actionable listening. That means finding out what your customers' "pain points" are and solving them in as many ways as possible. That means solving them with informational articles and blog posts. That means solving them with ebooks and white papers. That means solving them on your website with relevant and valuable content.

Doing all these things and mixing them up in the right way, positions you as the expert in your industry. It gets people interested in you. It draws them in. It makes engagement possible.

And the funny thing is, this is exactly how I met Lauren in the first place. Lauren creates great content all the time in multiple formats, so much so that I started to pay attention to her. Lauren understands the marketing formula for creating attention, interest and engagement with your customers. Isn't that what we all want?

There is no silver bullet and there is no one thing, but by reading this book, you'll be able to figure out which ingredients, working together in the right way, will help you attract and retain customers for the long term. Enjoy the book!

Joe Pulizzi

Co-Author, "Get Content, Get Customers, and Managing Content Marketing"

Founder, Content Marketing Institute

Introduction:
If you can't stand the heat...

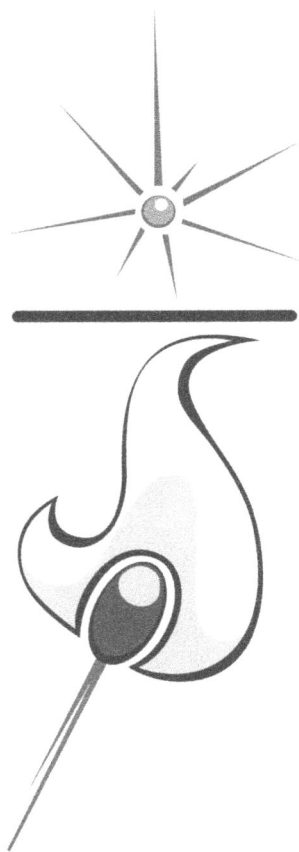

"Sometimes, we need a little fire lit under us to get us going and realize we are capable of doing fantastic things."

– Lauren Young

When I was in first grade, I had an abnormal fear of math. At the sound of the bell ringing to signal the end of our history session and the beginning of multiplication and division, I longed to disappear into a far away land I'd discovered in my social studies textbook.

We had these "emergency math drills" that used to make my stomach do loop-de-loops. A stark white piece of paper was placed on everyone's desk. Still warm from the ditto machine, the fumes of the purplish ink on the paper nauseated me further than the fact that I had 2 minutes to answer the 25 math questions on the paper. So I did what any normal child would do, I asked...

"Mrs. Mintz, can I use the bathroom?

It's an emergency."

I got out of it every time. That is, until it was report card day. My parents couldn't understand how I could do so well in all my subjects except for math.

A sampling of my math assignment grades looked like this for the first two semesters:

D, C, F, B, C, C, A, B, D, A, F, C, B, D, C, C, C, D, B, C

> **I was the picture child for inconsistency (or ADHD as some call it today) and a solid, below average, "D" student.**

My mother, who went to college to become a mathematician, made it her personal goal to spend evenings with me going over various examples, tactics and tips to remember how to approach a problem.

She knew if I could score A's and B's on some assignments, I could do it on all assignments. So I was given a challenge. If I brought my math grade up, I could finally have an Easy Bake Oven.

This was a $20 oven with a little heat lamp that baked tiny cakes and delicious desserts made with the cake mix packets that came with the oven. The mixes even came with icing that you could use to decorate your cake once cooled. The Easy Bake Oven was THE only thing missing from my life at eight years old.

Not long after the gauntlet was thrown, a sampling of my math assignment grades looked like this:

C, B, B, A, B, A, A, B, C, A, A, A, A, A, A, A, A, A, A, A

And I got my Easy Bake Oven.

What drives you to excellence? Sometimes, we need a little fire lit under us to get us going and realize we are capable of doing fantastic things. At 8, it was an Easy Bake Oven for me. At 16, it was a full college scholarship. At 24, it was freedom from a cubicle for the rest of my life. When we work a little harder toward our goals, it makes the reward that much sweeter.

All right, hot shot. Let's get moving!

What You Can Gain from the Right Ingredients

"When it's good, then it's good,
it's so good till it goes bad..."

– P!nk, music artist

"Ooh, I don't think this mayo
is any good. How long does it
usually take for this to go bad?"

– question posed by a new
Subway sandwich artist during
the lunch rush

Have you ever offered to cook for a potential significant other soon after you started dating? You are still in the "I want to impress you" stage and you want to make sure the food you prepare is delicious.

When I first cooked for my now husband, I was on his turf. It was a disadvantage from the start because I was working in an unfamiliar kitchen. I didn't know where the cookware was, or if he even had cookware. I didn't know how fast his stove would heat up and there was limited space for the prep dishes.

However, the meal still was amazing because all of the right ingredients were in place. I think my future husband enjoyed watching me flutter about the kitchen, opening and closing cabinets, furiously mixing batter and trying to convert quarts to pints or cups as the pasta nearly boiled over. I not only won him over with my chicken cacciatore, I won him over with my ability to be successful despite outside factors I couldn't control.

Likewise, when marketing a business, you also need to start with the right ingredients to win over your audience. There are three steps to follow. You can remember them by the acronym ECE

Exposure

Credibility

Engagement

EXPOSURE – *"I see you"*
Exposure is defined as marketing that is done purely to get people to remember your name. Are you familiar with Empire Today? It started out as Empire Carpet in 1959 in a Chicago suburb. The commercials aired daily, showcasing the Empire Man (the late Lynn Haudren) with the ubiquitous jingle "588-2300, Empire!" at least once during the morning news and again during the afternoon soap operas.

As the brand expanded to more than carpet and well beyond the Chicago area, the jingle was updated to "800-588-2300, Empire Today!" Over time, this brand was able to take root in advertising history as an example of how a great jingle can remain within the memories of our society for a lifetime.

Exposure is not limited to television commercials and radio jingles, but they definitely help. You can also gain exposure for your brand through the use of print advertising, outdoor advertising, Internet advertising and the ever popular and still necessary press release.

How to gain exposure quickly

- Write an article that is featured in your local newspaper

- Sponsor a charitable event

- Win an award

- Appear on television during a morning news show

- Contribute a column to a magazine

- Publish a book

How to lose exposure quickly

- Ignore industry trends

- Stop connecting with your local community

- Neglect to maintain a professional Web site

- Stop talking to your customers

- Offer no original content to your audience

- Fail to update your social media profiles

Once you reach a fair amount of exposure you achieve brand recognition. And isn't it all about recognition these days? The companies that are most often recognized are the ones you recall when it's time for you to make a purchasing decision.

After your business has reached maximum exposure to generate brand recognition, it's time to move on to the second step, which is...

CREDIBILITY – *"I like you"*
What does it take to get potential customers to like you? Did all tickets to a luncheon sell out when people discovered that you were delivering the keynote? Did you deliver a service above one's expectations? Did you offer "**lagniappe**" in the shipping box with their order? Or, maybe something went awry and you fixed the error at no additional cost...

All this leads the way to getting credibility.

> If you have an
> excellent product or
> an unmatched service,
> you could easily be out
> of business in three to
> six months if no one is
> talking about it.

The best customers are not the ones who just show up to appointments on time, tip well, or even send you a nice holiday card – your best clients bring you up in conversation all the time. Your best customers attend events where your target market convenes and they make a strong recommendation for your expertise. And, your best clients know how to make a powerful introduction between you and a potential new client.

Have you ever watched the Looney Tunes episodes featuring Wile E. Coyote and the Road Runner? Try as he might, Wile E. could not capture that Road Runner, and his supplier of choice, the Acme Corporation, was partially to blame.

The defective equipment became a running joke in the cartoons, as the audience knew the inevitable outcome of using shoddy equipment and Mr. Coyote remained optimistic (or naïve, whatever you prefer).

Imagine if Wile E. Coyote purchased these items and they backfired on him today. Would he detail his experiences on Facebook, or Twitter, or would he chalk it up as another loss? What would this do to the credibility of the Acme brand? If it's a large company, maybe not too much, but if there are enough customers complaining about the products, the business may begin to suffer until these problems are addressed.

The obvious solution in Mr. Coyote's case would have been to take his business elsewhere. Back in the 1940s (when Looney Tunes first debuted these characters), most people weren't doing much comparison shopping. Hate it or love it, they patronized certain stores because those stores carried what they needed. This created the "I need you, but I don't have to like you" form of brand loyalty. This means, you are the only game in town or the only vendor your customers know of. But, watch out.

As soon as someone else enters your market and can replicate your service with better customer service or at a lower cost, kiss your biscuits adios.

What You Can Gain from the Right Ingredients

How to gain credibility quickly

- Deliver on your product or service

- Network with professionals and industry leaders

- Receive an endorsement from a trusted public figure

- Love the work you do

- Volunteer in your community

- Contribute something dynamic to the world

How to lose credibility quickly

- Make promises you don't always keep

- Hand out business cards before a meeting begins

- Hand out business cards like a Vegas dealer

- Visibly hold a stack of business cards when entering a room

(Seeing a trend here?)

- Show up without showing up – you hear, but don't listen

- Fail to make a positive impact anywhere

Ok, I'm stepping off my soapbox about the business cards. This shameless self-serving manner of promotion is annoying to many entrepreneurs and a quick way to determine who is networking to build relationships and who are the sharks that only love to talk about themselves.

If you've made it this far, it's time to put the icing on top and make your newfound fans arrive early to your store and form a line down the street, "**Apple-style**"...

ENGAGEMENT – *"I want you"*

If there's something you really want, nothing can stop you from getting access to it. Remember my story about the Easy Bake Oven when I was eight? The idea of being able to bake individual cakes in a toy that resembled a colorful microwave was enough to help me overcome a crippling fear of math.

However, the significance of this story still remains to be revealed...

I am the oldest of four children, each roughly 24 months apart in age. Growing up that meant lots of sharing. Sharing a room, sharing toys, sharing a peanut butter and jelly sandwich - and if I tried to cut the sandwich unevenly, I heard a lot of whining and tattling. The list goes on and on.

I didn't mind sharing, but sharing four ways was not always fun.

Is it even worth eating the last Twinkie if you knew you could only have a quarter of it?

It was only about the size of my mom's tiny palm to begin with!

The allure of the Easy Bake Oven was that it made *individual* cakes. No need to share, just make enough cakes for everyone! The idea that I could enjoy a delicious treat all my own was enough to make me focus on my math and bring up my grades.

This dynamic continued with the Book It! reading program in fourth grade. We could receive a coupon for a free individual pizza at Pizza Hut if we read a ridiculous number of books within a semester. I loved to read, so it wasn't even a challenge for me to get the coupon. The challenge was to get my father to drive me to Pizza Hut once a week to pick up an individual pizza after fighting rush hour traffic to get home. As I write this, I can still hear him letting loose with expletives and it makes me smile…

Today, a column in a prominent business magazine and at least one Clio Award has replaced the Easy Bake Oven and individual pan pizzas. However, the desire to have something all my own still lingers in my mind.

Are you able to create the same type of desire in your customers for your product or service?

How to engage customers quickly

- Step from behind the counter (or computer) and introduce yourself

- Offer something that is invaluable

- Embrace innovation and take risks with your business

- Ask for feedback and LISTEN

- Thank them for their continued patronage

- Publicly recognize their contributions to your business

How to disengage customers quickly

- Make too many changes to your brand too quickly

- Push unwanted products and services under the guise of a "promotion"

- Go overboard with the emails, postcards, brochures and tchotchkies

- Look at your customer base as solely a revenue stream (they will know)

- Have a terrible Web site (or no Web site at all)

- Become aloof to practicing exemplary customer service

Engaging your customers is the most critical thing you can do. You can have exposure and credibility all day long, but if there is no engagement between you and your customers, they have no incentive to buy. To entice a customer to buy, you need to know how your customers will respond to you, based on the persona you have projected into their minds. In this case, you should care about what people think of you. I'm introducing a secret plan to the world in my next chapter, so don't put down this book!

How Do I Know If I Have the Right Ingredients?

Can I go on my way without you? How can I know? If I go on my way without you, where would I go?

– The Isley Brothers, "Voyage to Atlantis"

How Do I Know If I Have the Right Ingredients?

When you bake a pie from a recipe, have you ever noticed you are given a separate option based on the type of crust you want? For crispy crust, do X, Y and Z. For a flaky crust, try L, M, N, O and P. Your options may include everything from adding more ingredients to setting the oven at a different temperature.

As you begin to compose your marketing strategy, it is important to determine the type of persona you would like to project to your customer base.

EXPOSURE

you know them (+)   they know you (-)

| CREDIBILITY | they dislike you (-) | RENEGADE (+/-) Quadrant #4 | STAPLE (-/-) Quadrant #3 |
| | they love you (+) | EXPERT (+/+) Quadrant #1 | ELITIST (-/+) Quadrant #2 |

This is the FBC Matrix®. My company, Freshly Baked Communications, has used this internal tool to determine the appropriate tactic to use in marketing the companies of our clients...until now.

For the purpose of this book, we are introducing this matrix to the world. It helps answer the following questions:

- I know who my target market is, so why aren't my sales strong?

- My business satisfies an unmet need in the market, so where are the buyers?

- Will my price point alienate too many consumers?

- What do I need to do to create brand loyalty?

The four quadrants of this matrix represent the way customers will classify your business.

"Exposure" is reflected on the x-axis as either **you know them** (you understand your customers) or **they know you** (your customers have heard of your company). If **you know them,** this is positive for your brand, because you are able to tailor your products and services effectively to their needs. If **they know you,** this could be either positive or negative for your brand.

Why?

This is because you are known for being great or known for being terrible, or worse, indifferent.

It's not enough just to be known.

The focus of your business should not be to create a name for yourself.

You must satisfy an unmet need in the market. The only way you are able to do this is by studying consumer behavior. What do they like? What do they dislike? How often will they seek out your products and services? What are they currently using? Would your product or service save them time, money and effort (or all three)?

If you can relate to your customer base better, your sales will reflect your success and you can unequivocally say that you know them.

"Credibility" is reflected on the y-axis as either **they dislike you** or **they love you**. Pretty self-explanatory isn't it? If **they dislike you,** there are probably some changes you need to make in your company. If **they love you,** you're doing well, but you should continue to study their behavior to make sure they don't cheat on you with another brand.

Consumer brand loyalty is monogamous, and it is nearly impossible to sway a consumer from a brand that they love.

My mother buys Tide detergent, because she believes "it is the best." As the price of this brand increased over the years, she did not switch to a bargain brand or even complain about the cost. She continued purchasing it without a word because it "works every time." How nice would it be for your customers to feel this way about your brand?

So we have **E**xposure, and **C**redibility...we're missing one!

Or are we?

The entire matrix encompasses the presence of **E**ngagement. All companies that can be classified in this matrix have engaged their customer base in one form or another.

Take a look:

A pub in the business district provides the best "happy hour" deals in a 10-mile radius, but the wait staff is terrible. As a result, many people drive out of their way to a more welcoming spot for drinks – **Renegade**

You are running out of gas on the highway, and you see that the next rest stop features a Cheapy-Cheap Gas station, which is known for low-grade gasoline that you would prefer not to put into your BMW. Your car will not make it to the next stop 47 miles away, so you reluctantly merge to the exit ramp – **Staple**

A local clothing boutique is known for exclusive, one-of-a-kind pieces that always look great on you. At least twice a month, you stop in to check out the new offerings and usually end up spending a minimum of $300 during each trip. However, you have never received anything extra from the store other than a "thanks for stopping by" from the sales consultant as you exit. – **Elitist**

Your company promotes an event to your customers to receive a discount off your products and contribute to a local charity. The event sells out in one day and all registered attendees arrive at the event. A considerable amount of money is raised for the charity and your customers enjoy their experience and thank you for inviting them to attend. – **Expert**

If you have not engaged your customers, your business will not be featured in this matrix. You are considered an **unknown**. All companies that are just starting out (without the assistance of social media and/or PR) are unknown. All companies without a consistent brand image are unknown. And, all companies who are not using marketing to connect with their current and potential customer base are unknown.

If you were to do some **recon** in your industry to figure out who the most influential business owners are, would you appear as one of the "**top 5 answers on the board?**"

Unfortunately, if you remain unknown, you cannot remain in business.

> **If you fit within any of these quadrants, you can still be in business because you evoke an emotion from potential and existing customers.**

For example, the Renegade pub may have what I consider the best microbrews in the state, so I will wait a little longer to be seated during happy hour. I am *peeved* at the delay, but I am always *satisfied* with the drinks.

Or, the Elitist boutique may not distribute loyalty coupons or special shopping events, but the sales consultants steer me to fabulous, luxurious pieces that match my style better than any department store offering. I am *hopeful* that one day my frequent retail therapy sessions will pay off, but I remain *satisfied*. It's all about satisfaction.

In some cases, the customer perception of the company may have placed them within one quadrant, but it is not the right place for the company to be. Could you imagine if Harry Winston started advertising in the weekly coupon mailer? Yikes!

Here are the answers to the matrix questions from the beginning of the chapter:

👓 I know who my target market is, so why aren't my sales strong?

Hey Renegade, you may know who they are, but they don't like you. Time to change up your marketing strategy.

👓 My business satisfies an unmet need in the market, so where are the buyers?

Oh, the life of an Elitist. You are well known, but you are promoting your business to the wrong crowd. Are you willing to adapt your promotional tactics to survive?

👓 Will my price point alienate too many consumers?

Doesn't matter if you are a Staple. Consumers need you, until you are replaced by a low-cost alternative. Watch your back...or just modify your approach now.

👓 What do I need to do to create brand loyalty?

Just stay ahead of the trends and keep your customers happy. As an Expert, you cannot become relaxed. If you do, that is when your competition can (and will) move in on your territory.

Which companies have successfully made the transition from Renegade/Staple/Elitist to Expert? Here are some examples:

Ex-Renegade turned Expert – Apple

In the good ole days (or the bad ole days if you're a Baby Boomer or Gen Xer), I could only remember seeing an Apple in schools. They were odd, moved very slowly and were only good for playing Oregon Trail during Computer Lab class. The Compaq Presarios, HPs and Dell PCs ran the market until the colorful iMacs were introduced followed by a slew of other advanced portable machines from

Apple. The company realized people liked variety and the freedom to do whatever they wanted, from listening to any song they've ever heard on demand to reading the new best-seller without having to step foot in a bookstore.

Ex-Staple turned Expert – Arista/Interscope/Motown

These music labels used to charge exorbitant amounts for an entire album that only had 2-3 decent songs until the advent of Napster, LimeWire, Ares and a variety of other file sharing sites. They wised up and started offering just about any song on an album as a single via iTunes, Rhapsody and Amazon. Although their industry still struggles, they did listen to the voice of their consumers and gave them **what they want, what they really, really want.**

Ex-Elitist turned Expert – Tiffany & Co.

Tiffany has been the standard of status in the world for many years. Seeing the robin's egg blue is enough to bring women to tears, especially when it is presented to them with a pearl white bow (or claret red during the holidays) expertly tied around a palm-sized gift box. Seeing an opportunity to make Tiffany more relevant than the famous opening scene of the Audrey Hepburn film, "Breakfast at Tiffany's," the company began advertising the "Return to Tiffany" sterling silver bracelets, chokers and earrings at affordable price points in women's magazines. Wearing the pieces meant that any suitor worthy of your hand in marriage must return with you to Tiffany for an engagement ring. Today, it is difficult to find a woman who does not own one of the pieces from the "Return to Tiffany" line.

It is important to note that Elitist is not restrictive of only upscale or expensive brands.

The Elitist attitude can transfer to discount brands, as well.

It shows indifference to or unfamiliarity with their current and potential customer base.

EXPOSURE

you know them (+)   they know you (-)

	EXPOSURE	
CREDIBILITY — they dislike you (-)	**RENEGADE** (+/-) Quadrant #4	**STAPLE** (-/-) Quadrant #3
CREDIBILITY — they love you (+)	**EXPERT** (+/+) Quadrant #1	**ELITIST** (-/+) Quadrant #2

To reach a quadrant in this matrix is an achievement, because one of the most difficult tasks in business is to engage people. But, as Seth Godin mentions in his book, "The Dip," your status is relevant only in the eyes of your customers. The favorite brand of a suburban housewife could be different from region to region, city to city and household to household.

Yes, that makes it so much more difficult to isolate the right customers for your brand. The trick is to understand what influences people on a wide scale and use these methods (ingredients) to keep their attention. Go to the next chapter if you want to learn what successful brands have known for centuries!

How to Find the Right Ingredients

Do not believe in anything simply because you have heard it.

Do not believe in anything simply because it is spoken and rumored by many.

Do not believe in anything simply because it is found written in your religious books.

Do not believe in anything merely on the authority of your teachers and elders.

Do not believe in traditions because they have been handed down for many generations.

But after observation and analysis, when you find that anything agrees with reason and is conducive to the good and benefit of one and all, then accept it and live up to it.

– Buddha

"Ditto"

– Patrick Swayze in "Ghost"

How to Find the Right Ingredients

We are very predictable. Don't think so? Read the statements below and give yourself a point for each one that makes you say "yes."

We go to work.
We go home.
We work to afford our homes or save enough to enjoy a nicer home.

We have children.
We love our children.
These children influence our behavior, attitudes and priorities.

We have pets.
We love our pets.
These pets influence our decision-making abilities.

We like to go on vacation.
But we like to earn a living more.
We need a mental break from work.
We are willing to invest a considerable amount in home entertainment.

We like to eat.
We like to eat different things.

We get sick.
We prefer not to go to the doctor.
We avoid medical procedures unless a major influence advises us otherwise.

We like to drive our cars.
We also like to compare our cars to other people's cars.

We are curious about how others perceive us.
We also like to compare ourselves to others – especially public figures.

If you say "yes" to at least 12 of these statements, you are capable of being marketed to. You are able to be influenced by marketing and likely to base a purchasing decision on excellent positioning and promotion -whether you are aware of it or not.

Does that scare you? It shouldn't. Don't worry. Subliminal marketing was ruled ineffective back in the 1950s and 1960s, but emotional marketing is prevalent today. Corporations that employ savvy and highly educated marketing consultants and agencies use strategies and tactics based on various statements such as the ones on the previous two pages to capture as many consumers as possible.

The rest of this chapter will reveal the types of advertising you may have seen that offer some validation of these statements. I will caution that after reading this, you may experience heightened awareness of marketing tactics around you and it will be overwhelming. If this happens, hop in your Audi, drive to your nearest Walgreens and purchase some Aleve before continuing. Just kidding, just wanted to see if you would catch that...

We go to work.
We go home.
We work to afford our homes or save enough to enjoy a nicer home.

Work is not seen as an enjoyable place to be. How many fast food commercials do you see with men and women dressed in business casual, hunched over a wood laminate desk in a restrictive gray cubicle, finishing up the last of a detailed report, when some jerk leans over their space and snatches their lunch.

DISCLAIMER: You deserve to have your lunch snatched if you have it so prominently displayed and beautifully laid out on your desk. If this was not a food commercial and studio artists did not position the food in such a way, your smushed burger-n-fry combo would not be as appealing to your co-workers.

However, we can all relate to this situation because we rarely have privacy at work. At the end of the day, we commute home and lock the doors to enjoy our privacy again. We have to get up and go to work each week to afford the home we have.

> **If we are looking to save and buy a nicer home, perhaps we are not going to Fatty McGreasies for lunch and we are bringing a paltry Soup for One or carton of yogurt to work.**

We all know this is barely enough food to sustain us through our monthly status meetings. But the commercials promoting such products feature likeable characters with hair that holds up past 3 PM who are happily spinning around in their ergonomic chairs, clutching their spoons and staring into the fluorescent light, dreaming of their new home (or the end of the day).

We have children.
We love our children.
These children influence our behavior, attitudes and priorities.

If my child wrote all over the wall with markers, spilled grape juice all over the counter or dropped a pot of spaghetti across my hardwood floor, do you think my natural response would be, "Geez, I'm glad I stocked my cellar with Bounty, because it's the Quicker Picker-Upper!"? No, it wouldn't be. And if my husband is reading this, please take me in for an evaluation if this ever occurs.

We love our kids, but they can make us want to hide in a corner sometimes. I have no children at this time, but I have a 4-year-old niece who is adorable and precocious as the day is long. But all of her energy can be overwhelming. Of course children are going to knock over food and drink, and damage some walls, floors and other hard-to-replace portions of a home.

You have to be prepared!
Bounty will prepare you!
Get to the store post-
haste and purchase 17
rolls before it's too late!

If you see enough advertising warning you to be proactive about the actions of your children, you may notice that you have subconsciously shown a preference to one brand of paper towels, dish detergent, or diapers over another.

We have pets.
We love our pets.
These pets influence our decision-making abilities.

Puppies with one paw raised and their head tilted to the side while offering the slightest whimper can melt the hearts of red-blooded Americans everywhere. Kittens that sweetly walk across our laps and place their tiny paws on our newspaper or iPad while we are reading also make us smile.

Brands that are trying to appeal to your sensitive core will almost always have an advertisement that features a family pet. After all, they are family members, too. My Aussie Shepard/Border Collie mix, Devereaux, is a mainstay in regular conversation with me. His intelligence, willingness to follow instructions and charming personality delight my family and our guests.

As a matter of fact, just this minute he brought his treat ball into my office and rolled it next to my feet. He's really asking me to take his breakfast out of his traditional bowl and place it in the treat ball, so that he can chase it around the floor. And I have to oblige him because he's sitting here with one paw raised with his head tilted ever so slightly to the right.

How to Find the Right Ingredients

We like to go on vacation.
But we like to earn a living more.
We need a mental break from work.
We are willing to invest a considerable amount in home entertainment.

Can you hear the Bob Marley music in the background while you are sunning on a beach of white sand and reaching into a bucket of chilled Coronas? You can? Okay, now open your eyes and finish that logistics report and be quick about it.

We are always dreaming of an escape from our jobs, but we have mortgages and car notes and utility bills and college tuition to pay off.

> **At the end of a pay period, if we have enough to not order off the value menu, we're ahead of the game.**

That being said, our homes are the ultimate getaway during the week. We stock our homes with state-of-the-art technology, purchase Netflix subscriptions, learn the latest dances through Dance Central on Xbox Kinect and host dinner parties to have a reason to open a couple of bottles of wine on a Wednesday night - and not feel bad about it.

If you have people in your home, you must improve your furnishings, and this is proven by the furniture advertisements with four men celebrating as they jump off the leather sectional. They are spilling popcorn and pretzels as they watch their favorite team intercept the ball and make a touchdown. On the other half of the page, a nuclear family of four with the standard adult Golden Retriever all smile at the camera together while sitting on the same sectional. And who doesn't love multifunctional pieces?

We like to eat.
We like to eat different things.

Not much to say about this...if you're in the mood for different foods, scroll through a commercial break on your DVR during primetime television and discover what chipotle bacon, deep-fried fare sprinkled over pasta is available at your neighborhood family-friendly restaurant.

Sound disgusting? Millions of people would try it and one hundred things just like it (ever seen "Man vs. Food?"). Why do you think McDonald's doesn't stick with the Big Mac, large fries and Coca-Cola as their only offerings?

We get sick.
We prefer not to go to the doctor.
We avoid medical procedures unless a major influence advises us otherwise.

If you are unemployed, you know health insurance is really expensive. If you are employed, getting into the doctor is difficult and the co-pays seem to rise each year. It's best to hop on WebMD, self-diagnose, run into your local drugstore, and clear the shelves of cold, sinus, and pain medicines, right?

We've all done it, because it takes some major intervention for many of us to finally walk into the doctor's office. Is it leftover childhood fear of getting a shot? It is fear of the unknown that we have an incurable and debilitating disease that was once featured on House? Whatever the case may be, a spouse or concerned friend is usually the one who gives us the ultimatum to **get thee to a physician** or it will be **off with thy head**.

Next, you have people sitting on their leather sectionals, looking depressed, until a friend hands them a pamphlet about the new wonder drug you should "tell your doctor about." Medical advertising usually shows a progression in the way an actor feels from the beginning of the commercial to the end. These commercials are also great about showing a supportive and smiling doctor that is not rushed and has all the time in the world to answer the patient's questions about the new mysterious medicine.

Their hope is that you will be blinded by the physician's megawatt smile and not pay attention to the very dangerous side effects that are quickly blurted out at the end of the commercial.

We like to drive our cars.
We also like to compare our cars to other person's cars.

We are curious about how others perceive us.
We also like to compare ourselves to others – especially public figures.

What does the car you drive say about you?

This is the most common thread in new car commercials. Car companies fight with each other in advertisements like they are the Jets versus the Sharks in "West Side Story."

Can't you see a commercial with the Mercedes-Benz flashing its headlights in one corner of the alley and hear the BMW on the opposite side rev its engine to accept the challenge?

We are very conscious of how we are perceived by others, and as much as we don't think it matters, it does. Every time you walk into a job interview or a department store, you are sized up. When you merge onto an entrance ramp of an expressway, you are getting sized up. You drive a Toyota because you are concerned about your gas budget. You drive an Audi because you want to enjoy a luxury car without driving the stodgy Benz or the overexposed BMW. You drive a red car because you want to get noticed. You drive a convertible because you want everyone to know that this is just your summer car and you can afford more than one vehicle.

Maybe these statements do not apply to you, but people do form opinions about you based on your vehicle. And each time we smile as the 1993 Toyota Celica putters by, we feel a little bit more secure about our 2003 Nissan Altima.

Take this a step further and think about how we compare ourselves to celebs...how does she have 12 children and snap back to pre-pubescent size and shape in a mere two months? How does he keep a 12-pack chest when TMZ catches him coming out of a bar at least five days a week? And most importantly, why can't that be me? It's all smoke and mirrors. I highly recommend reading Tina Fey's autobiography "Bossypants" where she explains the arduous task of going in for a magazine photo shoot. Beauty is never in the eye of the beholder, it's in the eye of your admirer. Better buy the new "Self Loathing Woman" magazine and go on a mission to get every beauty product and a modern-day girdle!

Pray that your face doesn't melt and you don't pass out from constricted airflow in your $375 skinny-minnie jeans as you try to flirt your way to the $100,000 engagement ring, as advertised on pg. 1,067 in the fall fashion issue.

Does it all make sense now? Hopefully, you don't feel as if you have been living in the Twilight Zone and corporations have control over you.

It's just the way we have always been and marketers can use every form of print, TV, online and outdoor advertising to tap into our inner desires. A full listing of these ingredients can be found in the Appendix and a full description of how to use them is up to you and your marketing consultant of choice. If you want to go it alone, read on to the final chapter.

Start Pouring!

Words do two major things: They provide food for the mind and create light for understanding and awareness.

– Jim Rohn, rags to riches motivational speaker

Short, sweet and to the point. I hope you have learned something about the methods of marketing a business from a customer's point of view. I also hope that you realized the most important thing is that marketing is non-negotiable when it comes to operating a business. It has to be done or you have no chance to grow.

When you decide to start a business, the thought process behind the establishment and promotion of your brand is where you should take the most time. Rebranding sucks, so it's best to get it right the first time.

Feel free to refer to the FBC Matrix® to decide how you want to be seen by the public. It's not bad to be a Renegade, Staple or Elitist, but it is great to be known as an Expert.

You have the secret ingredients, so it's time to start pouring and start engaging clients correctly. If you want to know how much of these secret ingredients to use, wait for the second installment of this series, *Stir*. But don't worry, the information in this book you are reading will keep you occupied until the next book launch. *Bon appétit!*

Know Your Ingredients

What Will You Use to Market Your Business?

Article Writing
a form of PR developed through your commentary in a newspaper, or informative articles in relevant newsletters or magazines, either print or online publications

Co-branding
partnering with an equally strong or stronger brand to open your brand up to their customer base

Content Writing
what you have to say in your advertisements, social media profiles, blog, print media and all other forms of media; should be a compelling and consistent message

Direct Mail
a way to put your image directly in the hands of your audience through print media that is sent by traditional postal mail and encourages a direct response

E-mail Marketing
announcements related to your business sent via the Internet to specific e-mail addresses; the messages should not be sent to individuals who have not agreed to receive your messages (will be considered spam)

Online Advertising
interactive promotion of a brand found on Web sites, may include pictures or just text; typically fee based

Presentations/Public Speaking
getting in front of a live audience to share information that provides a credible image for you, your products and/or services; requires confidence and knowledge of audience needs

Print Advertising
fee-based promotion of a brand usually found in magazines, newsletters and newspapers

Print Media
consists primarily of brochures, postcards, media kits and anything tangible that is easy to pass around and share; also a term for printed magazines

Promotions & Events
limited-time-only occasions to introduce your products and/or services to a wide audience

Public Relations (PR)
primarily a proactive method of getting the word out about you, your products or company; results show who said what about you, good press and bad press included

Radio Advertising
passionate appeal for your patronage with a well-written script, paid for and placed by your company

Search Engine Optimization (SEO)
building and writing a Web site with special keywords based on consumer's search engine behavior for your industry

Social Media/Blogging
posting information about your company on platforms designed to get people to offer their warranted (and sometimes unwarranted) opinions – most prevalent platforms include Facebook, Twitter and LinkedIn, in addition to Wordpress and Tumblr blogs

Sponsorship/Community Service
drawing attention to an event or worthy cause and offering the expertise of your company to help a non-profit with their goals; unselfish way to get PR

Video Marketing
adding moving pictures with sound to your Web site or presentations to explain the purpose of your business

Viral Marketing/Word of Mouth
the impact of your brand on a large audience, based on their values and beliefs and a willingness to share; can't be purchased

Web site Design
the look and feel of your virtual business card, usually the first point of contact between you and a potential customer

Creating Your Recipe Book

Brand Marketing Strategy Notes

Creating Your Recipe Book

Brand Marketing Strategy Notes

_____

_____

_____

_____

_____

_____

_____

_____

_____

_____

_____

_____

_____

_____

_____

_____

_____

_____

_____

_____

_____

_____

_____

_____

_____

_____

Creating Your Recipe Book

SEO Content Writing Notes

_____

_____

_____

_____

_____

_____

_____

_____

_____

_____

_____

_____

_____

_____

_____

_____

_____

_____

_____

_____

_____

_____

_____

Creating Your Recipe Book

SEO Content Writing Notes

_____

_____

_____

_____

_____

_____

_____

_____

_____

_____

_____

_____

_____

_____

_____

_____

_____

_____

_____

_____

_____

_____

_____

_____

_____

_____

Creating Your Recipe Book

Copywriting & Editing Notes

_____

_____

_____

_____

_____

_____

_____

_____

_____

_____

_____

_____

_____

_____

_____

_____

_____

_____

_____

_____

_____

_____

_____

_____

_____

Creating Your Recipe Book

Copywriting & Editing Notes

_____

_____

_____

_____

_____

_____

_____

_____

_____

_____

_____

_____

_____

_____

_____

_____

_____

_____

_____

_____

_____

_____

_____

_____

_____

_____

Creating Your Recipe Book

Social Media Notes

_____

_____

_____

_____

_____

_____

_____

_____

_____

_____

_____

_____

_____

_____

_____

_____

_____

_____

_____

_____

_____

_____

_____

_____

Creating Your Recipe Book

Social Media Notes

_____

_____

_____

_____

_____

_____

_____

_____

_____

_____

_____

_____

_____

_____

_____

_____

_____

_____

_____

_____

_____

_____

_____

_____

_____

_____

_____

Creating Your Recipe Book

_____

_____

_____

_____

_____

_____

_____

_____

_____

_____

_____

_____

_____

_____

_____

_____

_____

_____

_____

_____

_____

_____

_____

Acknowledgements

Books are never easy to write, but I would like to thank my family for being the inspiration for my book - Ahmed, Amelia, Jasmine, Sandy, Stephen & Rose. It was never a dull day in the home where I grew up, and the same holds true today when I go back and visit. Thanks to my newest family, especially Kristen and my niece Frankie, for your support and honest feedback, which is always appreciated.

Thanks to my business coach, Pamela Marte, for opening my eyes to the obvious and not so obvious about growing a business and for always being a great friend.

Thanks to Ben Olson for the fabulous design and artwork in this book. I knew when I started writing, Ben, that you would be the one to create something never seen before on a bookshelf.

Thanks to Marge O'Connor for her eagle eyes and perfecting the work of a writer, which is never a simple task.

Thanks to Joe Pulizzi for always supporting my initiatives and writing the best foreword I could ask for. Content marketers have to stick together!

Thanks to Jackie Camacho-Ruiz, PR extraordinaire and the motivation to get this book published. You were right. Being an author is the most amazing thing!

Thanks to everyone who has made Freshly Baked Communications what is today, especially Rieko Wada, the team members of "Project X" and the Greater O'Hare Association.

And to my husband, Laurence, thank you for encouraging me to break the mold so early in life in exchange for freedom and peace and happiness.

If I have missed anyone, I apologize, but remember, I have more books to come in this series ☺

Appendix

Freshly Baked Communications Speak

pg. 11 - "lagniappe" – a tasty Creole word used to refer to "a little something extra," such as adding an extra helping of gumbo on your plate or a complimentary appetizer to your dinner with friends. In business, it could be some free advice in hopes of signing on a new client.

pg. 14 - "Apple-style" – the manner in which scads of people wait patiently in line for an inordinate amount of time in hopes of being one of the first to purchase a shiny new iSomething-Or-Other, that will be obsolete in two days.

pg. 26 - "unknown" – a term used in the creative industry to refer to an agency without a strong presence. For example: "I heard Billion Dollar Agency 1, Billion Dollar Agency 4 and two unknowns are bidding for the Acme Corporation account."

pg. 26 - "recon" – shortened version of the word reconnaissance, which means to scout the behavior of your competition in a stealthy manner.

pg. 26 - "top five answers on the board" – a reference to the game show "Family Feud." Contestants may give a great answer, but if it was not mentioned from a sample of 100 random individuals, it is wrong.

pg. 28 - "what they want, what they really, really want" – a reference from the Spice Girls debut single, "Wannabe," off their 1996 album "Spice."

pg. 44 - "get thee to a physician" – a reference to the "Hamlet" quote, when he tells Ophelia to "get thee to a nunnery." His intentions are to express that he has reached his breaking point with her behavior.

pg. 44 - "off with thy head" – adaptation of a famous quote by the Queen of Hearts, in the Lewis Carroll novel, "Alice in Wonderland."

About the Author

Lauren Young is the CEO and Founder of Freshly Baked Communications, LLC (FBC), a brand marketing strategy + creative writing firm with locations in downtown Chicago and Schaumburg, IL. After working as an intern at the headquarters of Kraft Foods in Glenview, IL, at 19 years old, she was torn between the dynamics of the fast-paced corporate world and her passion for writing.

Eventually, writing won, and Lauren gained valuable creative and business perspective after working with marketing and brand management at Kraft for four years. In 2008, she launched her boutique firm to satisfy the needs of small and large companies that were without an affinity for original content writing. She incorporates precise business strategy with a little personality to offer a non-traditional approach to traditional marketing methods.

Lauren is the 2011 recipient of the Daily Herald Entrepreneurial Excellence Award for an "Early Stage" business; she placed in the top 3% in the Google Online Marketing Challenge; and received shiny Oscar-like statues from having her creative work nominated for awards from both the Association of Marketing Communication Professionals (AMCP) and the International Academy of the Visual Arts (IAVA).

facebook.com/laurenyoungwrites • twitter.com/lyoungwrites

pourstirwatchserve.com

POLIR

Psst...did you finish Chapter 2 yet?

Are you a Renegade, Staple,
Elitist or Expert?

Join the discussion online and connect
with your group on LinkedIn!

Visit LinkedIn.com and type
"Pour by Lauren Young"
in the search field for Groups.
Choose from the four options
and learn how other business owners
are achieving marketing success!

Connect with the author:

www.PourStirWatchServe.com

facebook.com/LaurenYoungWrites

twitter.com/LYoungWrites

Company Website: www.FBC-Chicago.com

Freshly Baked Communications™
✔*Your Collateral is Ready!*™

www.ingramcontent.com/pod-product-compliance
Lightning Source LLC
Chambersburg PA
CBHW031814190326
41518CB00006B/330